BITBAY

A DECENTRALISED MARKETPLACE

2014-2015-2016-2017
A CONCISE BITBAY HISTORY BOOK

BitBay—A Decentralised Marketplace

by Christopher P. Thompson

Copyright © 2018 by Christopher P. Thompson

Book Author by Christopher P. Thompson
Book Design by C. Ellis

ISBN—13: 978-1717162274
ISBN—10: 1717162274

BITBAY

A DECENTRALISED MARKETPLACE

2014-2015-2016-2017
A CONCISE BITBAY HISTORY BOOK

CHRISTOPHER P. THOMPSON

CONTENTS

INTRODUCTION

Since the inception of Bitcoin in 2008, thousands of cryptocurrencies or decentralised blockchains have been launched. Most ventures into the crypto sphere have not gone to plan as their founders would have hoped. Nevertheless, there are currently hundreds of crypto related projects which are succeeding.

This book covers the history of BitBay, an open-source, publicly distributed cryptocurrency. It was launched on the 10th November 2014. Since that time, there have been challenges which have been overcome. After the initial four founders left with the majority of ICO funds, David Zimbeck, and other eager investors, were committed to make BitBay a great success. A team of trusted people are responsible for its wellbeing. Major topics covered in this book include:

- Announcement of BitBay on Bitcointalk (NOVEMBER 2014)

- Initial coin offering occurred for four days (NOVEMBER 2014)

- BitBay Blockchain hard forked to proof of stake 2.0 (NOVEMBER 2014)

- Brand new BitBay coin logo design chosen (JANUARY 2015)

- First beta public release of the market client (MARCH 2015)

- BitBay development phase (2016)

- BitBay Blockchain hard forked to proof of stake 3.0 (JANUARY 2017)

- BitBay decentralised voting poll occurred (APRIL 2017)

- New revamped BitBay Roadmap unveiled (OCTOBER 2017)

- BitBay Blockchain hard forked to Exotic UI Spending (NOVEMBER 2017)

- All time high 2014/15/16/17 BitBay market capitalisation (DECEMBER 2017)

INTRODUCTION

To be specific, this book covers a concise chronological series of events from the 7th November 2014 to the 31st December 2017. During this time, BitBay has attracted growing interest from inside and outside the cryptocurrency space.

You may have bought this book because BitBay, BAY, is your favourite cryptographic blockchain. Alternatively, you may be keen to find out how it all began. I have presented the information henceforth without going into too much technical discussion about BitBay. If you would like to investigate further, I recommend that you read material currently available online at the official website https://bitbay.market.

If you choose to purchase a certain amount of BAY, please do not buy more than you can afford to lose.

Enjoy the book :D

WHAT IS BITBAY?

BitBay is officially described as decentralised software that uses unique unbreakable smart contracts. These serve to remove the need to trust third party entities by the utilisation of several features including, most importantly, Double Deposit Escrow (DDE) (see page 18). Users are free to conduct any type of transaction, peer-to-peer, using the native proof of stake 3.0 BAY cryptocurrency. Ultimately, it is a free-to-use, trustless, secure and anonymous service which allows anyone to buy/sell goods/services online without a middleman.

Similar to other cryptocurrencies, it allows the end user to store or transfer value anywhere in the world with the use of a personal computer, laptop or smartphone. Cryptography has been implemented and coded into the network allowing users to send BAY units of account through a decentralised (no centre point of failure), open source (anyone can review the code), peer-to-peer network. Cryptography also controls the creation of newly staked BAY units of account.

The Slogan used by the BitBay Community to market the project is:

"THE FUTURE OF FREE MARKETS"

WHY USE BITBAY?

BitBay permits users to create their own decentralised marketplaces in which they can trade anything with value. Tangible goods or digital services can be bought or sold without the fees normally associated with other centralised marketplaces such as eBay. Other reasons for using BitBay include:

- **Redefining Global Trade**: Unbreakable smart contracts ensure no one profits from dishonest behaviour.

- **Tried and Tested**: It has been in constant development since 2014.

- **Safe and Secure**: Innovative features make BitBay more resilient.

BitBay utilises innovative technological features to guarantee high security whenever a transaction takes place. They are described in more depth on pages 18 and 19. Most are outlined below:

- **Unbreakable Contracts**: risks from third party entities eradicated.

- **Double Deposit Escrow**: deposit made by both seller and buyer.

- **Decentralised Markets**: create your own peer-2-peer market.

- **Exotic Spending**: create time based contracts.

- **Decentralised Voting**: conduct a fraud free poll.

- **Anti-password-theft System**: protects users from hackers.

- **Multi-signature Wallets**: secure wallets with two passwords.

- **Tor and Proxy Options**: provide high anonymity for users.

- **Dynamic Peg (coming soon)**: provides price stability.

IS BITBAY MONEY?

Money is a form of acceptable, convenient and valued medium of payment for goods and services within an economy. It allows two parties to exchange goods or services without the need to barter. This eradicates the potential situation where one party of the two may not want what the other has to offer. The main properties of money are:

- **As a medium of exchange**—money can be used as a means to buy/sell goods/services without the need to barter.

- **A unit of account**—a common measure of value wherever one is in the world.

- **Portable**—easily transferred from one party to another. The medium used can be easily carried.

- **Durable**—all units of the currency can be lost, but not destroyed.

- **Divisible**—each unit can be subdivided into smaller fractions of that unit.

- **Fungible**— each unit of account is the same as every other unit within the medium (1 BAY = 1 BAY).

- **As a store of value**—it sustains its purchasing power (what it can buy) over long periods of time.

BitBay easily satisfies the first six characteristics. Taking into account the last characteristic, the value of BitBay, like all currencies, comes from people willing to accept it as a medium of exchange for payment of goods or services. Additionally, it must be a secure way to store personal wealth. As it gets adopted by more individuals or merchants, its intrinsic value will increase accordingly.

COIN SPECIFICATION

At the time of publication of this book, the BitBay coin specification was:

Ticker/Unit of Account: BAY

Time of Announcement: 7th November 2014 at 08:49:07 UTC

Block Number One Generated: 10th November 2014 at 13:36:36 UTC

Lead Developer: David Zimbeck

Hashing Algorithm: SHA-256

Timestamping Algorithm: Proof of Stake 3.0 (PoS 3.0)

Initial Number of Coins: 1,000,000,000 BAY

Nominal Stake Interest: 1-5% annually (depends on staking volume)

Block Time: 64 seconds (average)

Number of Confirmations: 10, maturity: 50

Minimum Stake Age: 2 hours (no maximum)

MILESTONE TIMELINE

7th November 2014	—BitBay announced on https://bitcointalk.org
10th November 2014	—First block timestamped to the BAY Blockchain
11th November 2014	—BitBay ICO began at 13:00 UTC
15th November 2014	—BitBay ICO ended at 12:00 UTC
15th November 2014	—First BitBay explorer at https://chainz.cryptoid.info
16th November 2014	—BitBay became active on www.coinmarketcap.com
18th November 2014	—Bittrex initiated the trading pair BAY/BTC
22nd November 2014	—BitBay Blockchain transitioned to PoS 2.0
12th December 2014	—Current official BitBay Bitcointalk thread created
29th December 2014	—Official BitBay Slack Channel launched

2015

7th January 2015	—Brand new BitBay coin logo design chosen
11th March 2015	—C-Cex initiated trading pairs BAY/BTC and BAY/USD
23rd March 2015	—First beta public release of the bespoke market client
28th March 2015	—First tangible item sold on the BitBay marketplace
5th April 2015	—All time high 2015 market capitalisation reached
25th May 2015	—Bleutrade initiated the trading pair BAY/BTC
17th October 2015	—Pay 2 Mail Giveaway began
23rd October 2015	—Pay 2 Mail Giveaway ended
29th November 2015	—Number of blocks timestamped surpassed 500,000

2016

3rd April 2016	—Market capitalisation surpassed US$500,000
5th May 2016	—A major announcement was posted
18th November 2016	—Official BitBay YouTube Channel launched

MILESTONE TIMELINE

24th November 2016	—Market capitalisation surpassed US$1,000,000
4th December 2016	—All time high 2016 market capitalisation reached
5th December 2016	—Market client version 1.24 released
18th December 2016	—Number of blocks timestamped surpassed 1,000,000

2017

7th January 2017	—Market client version 1.25 released
7th January 2017	—Core QT wallet client version 1.2 released
21st January 2017	—BitBay Blockchain hard forked at 00:01:52 UTC
13th February 2017	—BitcoinPRBuzz Press Release published
22nd March 2017	—Market client version 1.26 released
30th March 2017	—First official BitBay Decentralised Vote announced
4th April 2017	—Decentralised Voting Poll ended at 07:00 UTC
22nd April 2017	—Market capitalisation surpassed US$10,000,000
25th May 2017	—Market client version 1.27 released
17th July 2017	—Market client version 1.28 released
28th July 2017	—Cryptopia exchange initiated live BAY/BTC trading
1st October 2017	—Official BitBay Block Explorer went live
8th October 2017	—New BitBay Roadmap unveiled
24th October 2017	—UPbit exchange initiated live BAY/BTC trading
1st November 2017	—Market client version 1.29 (Exotic UI Spend) released
20th November 2017	—Official BitBay website revamped and launched
27th November 2017	—BitBay Web-Wallet Application released
30th November 2017	—BitBay Blockchain hard forked at 00:00:48 UTC
16th December 2017	—Market capitalisation surpassed US$100,000,000
19th December 2017	—All time high 2017 market capitalisation reached

BLOCKCHAIN

Every cryptocurrency has a corresponding blockchain within its decentralised network protocol. BitBay is no different in this sense. A blockchain is simply described as a general public ledger of all transactions and blocks ever executed since the very first block. In addition, it continuously updates in real time each time a new block is successfully mined.

The BitBay Blockchain has hard forked several times since the first block timestamped on the 10th November 2014 at 13:36:36 UTC. These were:

- Transition to proof of stake 2.0 on the 22nd November 2014.

- Transition to proof of stake 3.0 on the 21st January 2017.

- The "Exotic Spending UI" hard fork on the 30th November 2017.

As a means for members of the general public to view the blockchain, web developers have designed and implemented block explorers. They tend to present different layouts, statistics and charts. Some are more extensive in terms of the information given. Usual statistics include:

- **Height of block** —the block number of the network.

- **Time of block** —the time at which the block was timestamped to the blockchain.

- **Transactions** —the number of transactions in that particular block.

- **Total Sent** —the total amount of cryptocurrency sent in that particular block.

- **Block Reward** —how many coins were generated in the block (added to the overall coin circulation).

PROOF OF STAKE

Proof of stake is a timestamping method used by BitBay to secure the network protocol. It sustains decentralisation and validates transactions. Therefore, no third party needs to be trusted to verify, then add, transactions to the blockchain.

BitBay has always used some type of proof of stake as its timestamping method. It has transitioned twice to different types over the last few years:

- A transition from PoS to PoS 2.0 occurred on the 22nd November 2014.

- A transition from PoS 2.0 to PoS 3.0 occurred on the 21st January 2017.

At the moment, users of the market client are able to stake BAY units of account at a nominal rate of 1-5%. Users must also wait a minimum of two hours before receiving staked BAY. Proof of stake 3.0 was described as follows:

"1 billion plus 1% annual growth from soon to be POS3.0 stake reward. POS3.0 is much better than its predecessor. It enforces that no matter what 1% will be added to the coin supply - that's based on every coin staking. Since it's impossible for every coin to stake you earn more than 1% because you are reaping the reward that the current unstaked coins would be generating as well."

CORE FEATURES

UNBREAKABLE CONTRACTS

Commonly referred to as smart contracts, they are computer protocols which enforce a negotiation or verify a transaction without the need for middlemen (third party entities).

DOUBLE DEPOSIT ESCROW

It is a mechanism used to punish both the buyer and seller if either one fails to keep their promise. Both parties deposit a certain amount into a joint account and only receive these back when the transaction is mutually satisfied.

EXOTIC SPENDING

Permits the user to create time based contracts. BAY units of account can be programmed to return to their rightful owner after a predetermined time period. Also, it can be used to verify the ownership of documentation on the blockchain.

DECENTRALISED VOTING

Its major potential purpose is to work alongside the decentralised algorithm to regulate dynamic peg technology. Stakers will be able to cast their votes for either an increase or decrease of the number of BAY units of account in circulation.

NO HIGH TRANSACTION FEES

Unlike centralised systems, users won't be burdened by high fees. BitBay allows merchants to grow their businesses, especially those operating on extremely low margins.

CORE FEATURES

DECENTRALISED ANONYMOUS MARKETPLACES

BitBay is an environment in which users are not forced to adhere to set rules, as is the case with centralised systems. Users are able to buy/sell directly with each other without disclosing personal information. Hence, there are no risks to users having their identity stolen from an unsecure centralised server.

ANTI-PASSWORD-THEFT SYSTEM

Allows the user to input their password without clicking or typing. A virtual keyboard is used instead.

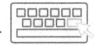

MULTISIGNATURE WALLETS

This features allows the user to create two separate keys stored in two separate locations. This means the wallet is effectively not hackable and extremely secure.

TOR AND PROXY OPTIONS

Options exist to provide the highest guaranteed anonymity of users via encrypted communication. No hacker will be able to read your communication, and use that to scam you.

DYNAMIC PEG (COMING SOON)

A decentralised solution to reduce the volatility risk usually witnessed in the cryptocurrency trading markets. Volatility can destroy commerce within a marketplace, so there will be a future feature to freeze or release BAY units of account to stabilise their value relative to the fiat US Dollar.

WALLET CLIENTS

A wallet client is basically a piece of software that can be used on a personal computer, tablet or other mobile device. It allows users to store BAY units of account as well as execute transfers with other users. Alternatively, it can be described as a means to access BAY units of account on the blockchain (public transaction ledger). The wallet software cryptographically generates and holds the public and private keys necessary to make transactions possible.

Four different types of wallet client are available:

- **BitBay Market Client** —the unique and bespoke BitBay wallet client. It permits users to benefit from many innovative core features.

- **BitBay Core QT Wallet Client** —a simpler wallet client which allows the user to send, receive, store and stake BAY units of account.

- **BitBay Web Wallet** —a standalone web-based application.

- **BitBay Android Mobile Wallet** —smartphone utilisation of BitBay.

BitBay Client

BitBay Wallet

CRYPTOCURRENCY EXCHANGES

A cryptocurrency exchange is a site on which registered users can buy or sell BAY units of account against other currencies. Some exchanges require users to fully register by submitting certain documentation including proof of identity and address. On the other hand, most exchanges only require users to register by creating a simple username and password with the use of an e-mail account.

BitBay has enjoyed the vast majority of live trading on Bittrex. The price of one unit of BAY account reached an all time high of 1,995 Bitcoin Satoshi on Bittrex on the 26th June 2017.

Seven exchanges have initiated live BAY trading over the years:

Exchange	Based	Traded Against	Date Initiated
Bter	China		15th November 2014
Bittrex	USA	BTC	18th November 2014
C-Cex		BTC	11th March 2015
Bleutrade			25th May 2015
Cryptopia	New Zealand	BTC	28th July 2017
UPbit	South Korea	BTC	24th October 2017
BarterDEX			6th February 2018

As can be seen above, a decentralised exchange added BitBay in February 2018. It allows people to execute atomic swap trades which involve no trusted middlemen to validate the trade. Blocknet, CoinSwitch and Indacoin have since added BAY.

BITBAY TEAM

A committed, devoted and energetic team from around the world are responsible for the BitBay project. Main core members are tasked with managing and organising the project. They are:

Name	Position	Based
David Zimbeck	Lead Developer	Mexico
Bjørn Alsos (Munti)	Operations Manager	Norway
Craig Claussen	Applications Manager	USA
Shorn	Project Manager	Spain
Aletha Kellond	Recruitment	England

As well as lead developer David Zimbeck, other people have been hired on a part or full time basis to help code BitBay:

Alex	Developer	Norway
Anoxy	Developer	Sweden
Slava	Developer	Russia
Chris	Developer	Spain
Stanislav	Developer	Ukraine

Three individuals have been hired to design graphics associated with the image of the BitBay Brand. They are responsible for making the project stand out from the rest of the crowd:

Giorgos Kontopoulos	Web Development & Design	Greece
Bruno Guimarães	Art Director	Brazil
Louise	Graphic Designer	England

BITBAY TEAM

Other team members are trusted to market the project on as many social media platforms as possible. Blogs, videos, conference speeches, articles etc. are important methods which can be used to increase BitBay adoption:

Luiz Yassuda	Social Media Manager	Brazil
Cory	Communications	USA
Matt	Technical Writer	USA
Mantrack	Community Support	France
Charlotte	Email Marketing	England
Leah Zitter	Content Marketing	USA
Elaine	Writer	
Anfree	GUI Design	
Fernando	SEO Specialist	Germany
Lowercase	Video	
GitGud	Security Expert	

Community managers have been hired from across the globe. Mohamed is in charge of all the other community managers. They are:

Mohamed	Communities Manager	Colombia
David	French Community Manager	France
Anmol	Indian Community Manager	Hong Kong
Igors	Russian Community Manager	Latvia
Seungjin Oh	Korean Community Manager	South Korea
Manuela Garcia	Spanish Community Manager	Colombia
Akio Sashima	Japanese Community Manager	Japan

COMMUNITY

A community is a social unit or network that shares common values and goals. It derives from the Old French word "comuntee". This, in turn, originates from "communitas" in Latin (communis; things held in common). BitBay has a community consisting of an innumerable number of individuals who have the coin's well being and future goal at heart. These individuals almost always prefer fictitious names with optional corresponding "avatars". Notable members of the community are David Zimbeck, Craig Claussen and Bjørn Alsos.

At the time of publication, there are social media sites (and other official websites) on which discussion and development of BitBay take place. These are:

- https://bitbay.market   (Official Website)

- https://t.me/bitbayofficial   (Official Telegram Group)

- https://twitter.com/BitBayofficial   (Official Twitter Account)

- https://bitbay.slack.com   (Official Slack Channel)

- https://forum.bitbay.market   (Official Forum)

Since the 12th December 2014, the following has been the official BitBay Bitcointalk forum thread:

- https://bitcointalk.org/index.php?topic=890531.0

In essence, the community surrounding and participating in the development of BitBay is the backbone of the coin. Without a following, the prospects of future adoption and utilisation are starkly limited. BitBay belongs to all those who use it, not just to the team who aid its progression.

A CONCISE HISTORY OF BITBAY

LIST OF CHAPTERS

I.   BITBAY ANNOUNCED ON BITCOINTALK ON 7TH NOVEMBER 2014

II.   FIRST BLOCK TIMESTAMPED ON 10TH NOVEMBER 2014

III.   ICO LASTED FOR NEARLY FOUR DAYS (2,765.72 BTC RAISED)

IV.   LIVE BAY TRADING COMMENCED ON BTER AND BITTREX

V.   TRANSITION FROM PoS TO PoS 2.0 ON 22ND NOVEMBER 2014

1

BITBAY ANNOUNCEMENT AND INITIAL COIN OFFERING

"BitBay is a suite of free-to-use, multi-platform applications including the world's first fully-functional Decentralized Marketplace."

As a way to announce BitBay to the wider cryptocurrency community, an officially recognised Bitcointalk forum thread was created on the 7th November 2014 at 08:49:07 UTC. It was initially titled "ANN:[BAY] BitBay |Decentralized Market-place|Smart Contracts|IoT Tech|ICO on Bter". It would serve as the main channel of discussion. Despite its creation, other social media platforms, as is usually the case, would be created. BitBay's major focus at the beginning was to supply the world with a completely unbreakable and decentralised marketplace. Ultimately, a system without the need for trusted third party entities was being sought after.

Core QT wallet clients had already been tested and were awaiting confirmation from a third party at https://www.cryptocertify.com. David Zimbeck, the lead developer from the beginning, was from BitHalo; the first person to release smart contract software which was then utilised in a cryptocurrency called Blackcoin.

An initial coin offering (ICO) was scheduled to take place very soon. The original founders decided to use a centralised Chinese cryptocurrency exchange called Bter to manage it. Besides this, a simple project roadmap was published:

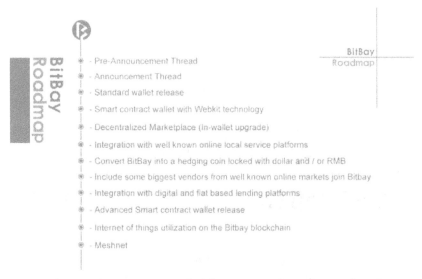

They wanted to under promise and deliver more than expected. There was overwhelming enthusiasm about the technology planned to be developed.

On the 9th November, the core BAY team unveiled how much each BAY unit of account would cost during the ICO. Early investors were able to purchase more BAY units of account for a certain number of Bitcoin Satoshi.

Day #	Date	Price per unit BAY (BTC Satoshi)
1	11th November	252-264
2	12th November	264-276
3	13th November	276-288
4	14th November	288-300
5	15th November	300

One unit of BAY account increased in price by 1 Bitcoin Satoshi (0.00000001 BTC) every two hours on the hour (UTC time).

Block #1 (Reward 0 BAY) November 10th 2014 at 01:36:36 PM UTC

Block #2 (Reward 1,000,000,000 BAY) November 10th 2014 at 01:36:38 PM UTC

As can be seen above, the first block of the BitBay Blockchain timestamped on the 10th November. The second block timestamped only two seconds later. Block number two generated the initial one billion BAY units of account ready to be distributed to potential ICO investors.

On the following day, the ICO began at 13:00 UTC. It was stated that all Bitcoin, BTC, raised would be held by Bter until the successful release of the core QT wallet clients. Unfortunately, this never materialised as planned.

Within the first forty hours of the ICO, over 1,000 BTC (~ US$450,000 on the 13th November 2014 at 05:00 UTC) had been raised. The initial founders were proud of the community's support and promised investors would not be disappointed.

On the 15th November, the ICO sold out approximately one hour before the scheduled 13:00 UTC end time. The total funds raised stood at 2,765.72 BTC or roughly US$1,080,000. On the same day at 22:00 UTC, live trading commenced on Bter. Core QT wallet clients for both Windows and Mac OS X were released thereafter. One comment was posted at the time:

> **"We would like to thank all our community and supporters**
> **and investors and friends for this success."**

On the following day, the first block to generate the very first staked BAY was timestamped:

Block #7,650 (Reward 0.36047291 BAY) November 16th 2014 at 09:26:17 AM UTC

This was also the day on which BitBay successfully became active on the cryptocurrency ranking website www.coinmarketcap.com. It primarily ranks cryptocurrencies in descending order of market capitalisation. Other statistics, charts and data are also accessible there.

On the 18th November 2014, Bittrex became the second cryptocurrency exchange to initiate live trading between BitBay and Bitcoin. Based and fully regulated in the USA, it began operations on the 13th February 2014 in beta testing mode. It exited beta testing mode on the 28th February 2014 as twelve cryptocurrencies and twenty one trading pairs went fully live. BitBay has enjoyed the vast majority of trading on this exchange.

A protocol change occurred on the 22nd November. The BitBay Blockchain successfully transitioned from PoS to PoS 2.0 at block number 20,000.

Block #20,000 (Reward 14.49270305 BAY) November 22nd 2014 at 11:14:36 PM UTC

This protocol change was deemed necessary in order to make the blockchain more secure, reliable and faster. Unlike the previous protocol, PoS 2.0 encourages nodes (computers) to stay online for those nodes to qualify for a stake reward. The more nodes continuously online, the less risk of future security issues.

During the next couple of weeks, David Zimbeck was "left holding the bag" as all four founders (Steven Dai, Robert Duskes, Ryan Wright and the owner of Bter Lin Han) abandoned the project. Besides this, they stole the majority of the ICO funds. It had become apparent that they brought David Zimbeck on board to increase the respectability of BitBay and to use his reputation. As a result, David became the only person whose responsibility it was to keep BitBay active. Despite this inconvenience and betrayal, he vowed to make BitBay a shining success.

A new official BitBay website at http://thebitbay.net launched on the 6th December. The following was posted:

"Thanks for all the great feedback on the new website layout guys. Don't worry, the layout guys will get the typos sorted. That will be part of the final run though. We just wanted to get an update and a few shots out to you guys today : -)"

Since the addition of BitBay to www.coinmarketcap.com, its market capitalisation had gradually decreased from just over US$1 million to about US$300,000. What follows are historical US Dollar prices of one unit of BAY account alongside corresponding US Dollar daily trading volumes and approximate daily average US Dollar market capitalisations:

	Low US$	Open US$	Close US$	High US$	Volume US$	Market Cap US$
16th Nov	0.001032	0.001032	0.001047	0.001050	35,871	1,032,480
23rd Nov	0.000992	0.001040	0.001049	0.001077	21,887	1,039,580
30th Nov	0.000797	0.000907	0.000867	0.000947	25,418	906,960
7th Dec	0.000410	0.000689	0.000524	0.000704	37,417	689,461
11th Dec	0.000257	0.000308	0.000257	0.000328	31,947	308,504

On the 8th December, the Bitcoin Satoshi price of 1 BAY went below 100 for the first time since records began on www.coinmarketcap.com.

Other events which occurred during this period included:

- On the 8th November, an official BitBay Twitter account was created at https://twitter.com/BitBayMarket/ (unofficial account).

- An AMA (Ask Me Anything) with David Zimbeck was hosted on Reddit for those who could ask questions before investing in the ICO. It happened on the 10th November at 19:30 UTC.

- On the 11th November, the first official BitBay website was launched at https://www.thebitbay.org/

- On the 15th November, a BitBay Facebook group, that turned out not to be very popular, was created.

- The first BAY Block Explorer went live at https://chainz.cryptoid.info/bay/ on the 15th November.

I. NEW OFFICIAL BITBAY BITCOINTALK FORUM THREAD CREATED

II. BITBAY SLACK CHANNEL LAUNCHED

III. NEW BITBAY LOGO CHOSEN VIA A COMPETITION

IV. C-CEX INITIATED BOTH BAY/BTC AND BAY/USD

V. TESTS CARRIED OUT ON BESPOKE MARKET CLIENT SOFTWARE

2

BITBAY REVITALISED
AND REBRANDED

"Everyone knows my original intention was to be project manager. However now, I've got many different things to work on in the code" - David Zimbeck

After the turmoil surrounding the initial four founders, sole developer David Zimbeck, and other eager investors, were motivated to drive the project forward. A new official BitBay Bitcointalk forum thread was created on the 12th December 2014 at 12:38:43 UTC titled "Official BitBay Thread |Decentralized Marketplace|Smart Contracts|IoT Tech". It can be accessed via the URL link immediately below. They had been locked out of the original thread.

https://bitcointalk.org/index.php?topic=890531

Other active social media platforms at this time were:

Facebook:	https://www.facebook.com/pages/BitBay-Project/1589213477978208
Google+:	ttps://plus.google.com/communities/114750118216930193130
Twitter:	https://twitter.com/BitBayProject

On the 29th December 2014, BitBay began to utilise a social media platform called Slack. It provides an organisational environment in which discussions can take place within different customised channels. BitBay Slack Administrator user "Lanthan57" publicly announced the website domain at https://bitbay.slack.com and invited community members to privately message him for a registered invite. BitBay were confident it would improve social and technical conversations.

Slack launched in August 2013 and was founded by Stewart Butterfield. The name is an acronym for "Searchable Log of All Conversation and Knowledge".

On the penultimate day of December 2014, work was underway to rebrand the BitBay coin logo. A competition began immediately and was scheduled to end on the 10th January 2015. A prize fund totalling 1,000,000 BAY (~0.6 BTC or ~US$315) had been set aside for the best three designs.

1st Prize: 500,000 BAY
2nd Prize: 300,000 BAY
3rd Prize: 200,000 BAY

Graphic designers were encouraged to make their designs public on the BitBay Bitcointalk forum thread for everyone else to see. A design brief was issued:

> "We are looking for something possibly abstract to represent BitBay which is both our currency, and also a decentralized service set that can enable blockchain based service, such as decentralized marketplace and decentralized smart contract applications.
>
> We are looking for something that can double as a logo for our decentralized service and a symbol for BitBay currency."

David Zimbeck assured the community that things take time and he was not going to rush to satisfy eager investors. Above all else, he politely insisted on patience.

On the 1st January 2015, David Zimbeck reminded the community he had limited time, so could not manage every single aspect of the project. He was willing to pay small bounties to talented individuals or other entities. He went onto say:

> "Everyone knows my original intention was to be project manager. However now, I've got many different things to work on in the code and it will be months before i can relax. I can give as much time as possible to work on project management but it comes second to coding."

Members of the community had been busy designing and publishing BitBay coin logos over several days. Some of the most interesting designs were:

user "funsponge"	user "EddyShark"
1st January 2015	1st January 2015

user "Gizfreak"	user "unusualfacts"	user "KC6TTR"
30th December 2014	3rd January 2015	3rd January 2015

On the 6th January 2015, user "issie81" posted the following two images:

Despite a previously set deadline for entries, the competition ended three days beforehand on the 7th January. David Zimbeck described the coin logo and corresponding font design (above) as excellent. He also said:

> "Ok so the community has spoken. The above logo wins, I will pick the runner ups and we will dispense prizes. If you can email me or PM a link to download the HQ logo, that would be appreciated. Will use this logo in the new release in a couple days."

As promised, David Zimbeck chose which coin logo deserved to win second and third prizes. He gave his input on the top three designs:

Winner (issie81) : This logo gave the feel of the original but in a more modern way. It was also well stylized and unique. The designer has a very good feel for branding. Good job! Also, the community all responded very positively about it. And the community is what its all about.

2nd prize (unusualfacts30) : All of your submissions were highly creative! And that counts for a lot. It is the people who are creative that always end up inventing new things because they are willing to take risks. And although your first submission would be more suited for a cool looking symbol than a logo, it was a really great looking design!

Third prize (EddyShark) : I'm a sucker for simplicity. All of your logos were professional. And although had we gone in this direction, we may have wanted to mess with the colors and style a bit, I liked the direction it was going.

David Zimbeck also personally tipped five other participants 50,000 BAY each who did not finish in the top three. Funsponge, spookycoins, Decentradical, KC6TTR and digicidal were all asked to send their wallet addresses via private message.

A bespoke market client was being tested ready for release. Members of the community who wished to test it were encouraged to directly contact BitBay Slack Administrator Jean Marc Hoffmann (also known as user "Lanthan57").

On the 16th January, the BitBay team (formed from ICO investors and other eager supporters) notified the community of two recently created social media accounts thanks to user "meta". The brand new coin logo design was incorporated into:

Facebook Page: https://www.facebook.com/bitbaymarket
Twitter Account: https://twitter.com/bitbaytalk (@bitbaytalk) CREATED: 14/01/2015

During February, BitBay team members replied to genuine concerns relating to slow progress and lack of regular updates. They admitted the launch back in November 2014 was not the smoothest. Other things they pointed out included:

- There was no control over the original social media accounts.

- It was difficult to know which core QT wallet clients were trustworthy.

David Zimbeck was submitting most of his technology updates on BitBay Slack where the team were spending most of their time. David was quoted as saying:

"I've tested posting orders to the markets and I can easily add and remove orders or markets. Now I am designing the whole UI and templates. That is the most complex part since each template will auto-execute or greatly assist you. I've got to decide how much customization I want with it before debuting the markets. Its possible I will give some updates with screenshots in the near future."

On the 11th March, an exchange called C-Cex initiated two separate trading pairs BAY/BTC and BAY/USD. It was the first exchange to offer cryptocurrency traders direct trading of BitBay against the US Dollar.

C-Cex opened their trading platform to the public in late January 2014.

I.   **FIRST BETA PUBLIC RELEASE OF THE MARKET CLIENT**

II.   **FIRST TANGIBLE ITEM SOLD ON THE BITBAY MARKETPLACE**

III.   **ALL TIME HIGH 2015 MARKET CAPITALISATION ON 5TH APRIL 2015**

IV.   **BLEUTRADE EXCHANGE INITIATED THE BAY/BTC TRADING PAIR**

V.   **SLOW PROGRESS DURING MAY, JUNE AND JULY 2015**

3

MARKET CLIENT
BETA RELEASED

"Say HELLO to the world's first decentralized markets!!" - David Zimbeck

On the 23rd March 2015, David Zimbeck enthusiastically announced the first public release of the bespoke market client in beta testing mode. It included many innovative features not present in the regular core QT wallet client. He emphasised it would go through innumerable changes before the final stable (not beta) release. Therefore, he advised users to exercise caution and expect turbulence, especially early on. Beta software is, after all, experimental.

David Zimbeck was happy to receive constructive feedback on its functionality, user friendliness and appearance. All members of the community were free to test it. As much input from beta testers was appreciated so as to speed up the process of finding bugs or flaws in the underlying code base.

Core QT wallet clients were still going to be released, because this was the only way allowing users to stake BAY units of account for the time being.

Market Client Beta Released

Since the 23rd March 2015, several items had been listed on the beta client marketplace. The first item successfully sold on the 28th March. It was purchased by David Zimbeck himself. User "rqdxrocket" said:

> "The first tangible item has now been sold on the market. My Good Year tire pressure gauge has been mailed off to the lucky buyer which just happened to be dzimbeck (David). The escrow was released back to me exactly like it was supposed to.
>
> Hopefully this can be remembered as the "10,000 BTC Pizza" except this will the called the "5990 Bay tire pressure gauge"
>
> Now I just need to make sure I figure in shipping and handling the next time I sell something. :-)
>
> Thanks Team BitBay"

A milestone in terms of price occurred on the 5th April. BitBay reached its all time high 2015 market capitalisation at roughly US$455,115. Corresponding prices of one unit of BAY account were US$0.000455 and 177 Bitcoin Satoshi. According to the website www.coinmarketcap.com, historical figures leading up to this day were:

	Low US$	Open US$	Close US$	High US$	Volume US$	Market Cap US$
2nd April	0.000197	0.000215	0.000248	0.000253	1,465	215,277
3rd April	0.000223	0.000248	0.000297	0.000300	1,723	247,970
4th April	0.000273	0.000297	0.000331	0.000361	2,608	297,641
5th April	0.000297	0.000331	0.000386	0.000455	5,513	331,655

Bitcoin Satoshi prices and corresponding BAY daily trading volumes on the top three recognised exchanges on the 5th April were:

	Low	Open	Close	High	Volume (BAY)
Bittrex	109	142	148	177	14,422,511.64
Bter	138	148	164	171	1,476,887.76
C-Cex	142	142	180	180	102,333.33

In response to some people who questioned why the BitBay team had not yet adequately marketed the project, the team said they had been focusing more on the technical aspects. The market client was still in beta testing mode and tests were being carried out to make sure it functioned as intended. They wanted to wait until the software had exited beta, before a massive marketing move. A quote from the team was posted:

> "Be aware that larger media outlets are not interested in reporting on unfinished work that people cannot properly use yet.
>
> And remember, true marketing is creating a product that the market wants, not pushing just anything down its throat!"

David Zimbeck invited interested parties to participate in promoting BitBay. He wanted people to design banners, diagrams and other relevant material.

On the 20th April at 11:01:08 UTC, David Zimbeck was quoted as saying:

> "Hey there guys, so im making lots of updates and wanted to let you all know, if there is anyone who is good with PR or knows bloggers or would like some articles please reach out to me or the slack group.
>
> Mostly, im usually busy coding so i dont have time to leverage my pr contacts. However, it would make sense for someone to reach out to a few bloggers or bitcoin pr news outlets to get some articles on the subject of decentralized servers and markets as well as pegging etc. I can always pay bounties for that as well.
>
> Thanks and hope you all are looking forward to the next round of updates."

Bleutrade was the fourth officially recognised cryptocurrency exchange to initiate the live BAY/BTC trading pair on the 25th May 2015. Unfortunately, trades of BAY units of account there did not become significant.

Throughout the remaining weeks of Spring 2015, a significant number of people perceived progress as sluggish. David Zimbeck hoped people understood that software development takes time. As he previously said, he did not want to over promise and under deliver. He was busy creating UI (user interface) templates for the bespoke market client. The source code had surpassed 30,000 lines!

There were others who continued to support David Zimbeck through these demanding times. A supporter posted the following comment:

> "David is working hard on the advanced BitBay client, fixing it up and adding more features and templates. This is indeed a huge task but we are seeing daily progress and things are really shaping up."

On the last day of July 2015, an update was posted on the official BitBay Bitcointalk forum thread. Several points covered were:

- David Zimbeck was working on new user interface templates which were planned to be released one by one for particular BitBay Slack members to beta test.

- A peer to peer (P2P) reputation system for the market client was being tested.

- Support for foreign languages was being implemented into the market client.

- Preparations were being made to launch an official BitBay forum.

- An in-built cryptocurrency exchange on the market client was being worked on (in alpha testing mode).

A growing number of people were joining the BitBay Slack Channel. It was viewed as the right place to stay tuned on project related news and meet fellow BitBay followers.

I.   **NEW BLOCK EXPLORER HTTP://BAY.EXPLORER.BITNODES.NET**

II.   **NEW OFFICIAL BAY WEBSITE LAUNCHED AT HTTP://BITBAY.MARKET**

III.   **FURTHER HELP REQUIRED FROM THE COMMUNITY**

IV.   **PAY 2 MAIL (P2M) GIVEAWAY TOOK PLACE**

V.   **BAY MARKET CAPITALISATION SURPASSED US$500,000**

4

BITBAY
DEVELOPMENT PHASE

*"We have done a lot of testing the last weeks, and so far we haven't found
any major problems. Thank you David for doing such a solid job."* - Bjørn Alsos

During the next several months, development of the project was busy behind the
scenes, but there were not many updates. Discussions were taking place primarily
on BitBay Slack, and posts on the official BitBay Bitcointalk thread were very sparse.

Aspects relating to security, speed, stability and user friendliness of the client
software were high priority. New updates were released after successful testing
phases. David Zimbeck and others were willing to help as many people as possible
to make sure they were running the most recent release.

During Summer 2015, two key updates were:

- The opening page of the official BitBay Bitcointalk forum thread was updated
  to include the latest download links for all relevant wallet clients.

- A new BitBay Block Explorer went live at http://bay.explorer.bitnodes.net/

In August, the new official BitBay website went live at http://bitbay.market. It incorporated the recently launched forum which would serve as another "great hub" for BitBay related information, updates, technical help and community adoption. Meta and Bjørn Alsos were praised for their hard work setting it up.

Also during Summer 2015, a "Buy/Sell Coins" template was ready for testing by BitBay Slack members. Another template called "Custom Contract" was also being tested. Prominent team members invited people to contact them, either on Slack or by e-mail at info@bitbay.market, in order to download it. Official download links were also provided at http://bitbay.market/getstarted/#

On the 6th October, David Zimbeck notified the community he had recently taken a break from coding to sort out some personal issues. Two weeks prior to this notification, Bjørn Alsos praised David by saying:

> **"We have done a lot of testing the last weeks, and so far we haven't found any major problems. Thank you David for doing such a solid job."**

A growing number of people were now contributing to the project. Nonetheless, further help from the community was required. It was in the best interest of investors to contribute, so as to protect their investment. Five suggestions were listed how people could help:

- To test and abuse the software. More testers equals a better chance to find flaws. Input of ideas to improve software also welcome.

- To market BitBay by writing articles or creating blogs.

- To translate the opening post of the official BitBay Bitcointalk forum thread into different languages.

- To fill the recently launched forum with guides and tutorials. They wanted this forum to become the "help desk" destination for BitBay.

- To say something appealing on one or more of the current BitBay social media and discussion channels.

On the 10th October, BitBay announced their intention to host a giveaway by utilising a relatively new feature of the market client called P2M (Pay to Mail). It was described as the first "big push" of marketing the project to a wider audience. P2M enables users of the market client to send/receive BAY units of account securely and quickly via e-mail. At this time, only a Windows compatible market client (version 1.21) was available. Users of this client had to register for it by sending 1 BAY to the campaign e-mail address p2m.campaign@google.com between the 10th and 16th October. Each registered participant was allowed a maximum of ten P2Ms with associated bounty rewards. It ran from the 17th October to the 23rd October.

It was effectively a campaign, open to anyone, to help spread the word about the potential of BitBay as a truly decentralised marketplace. Unfortunately, reception of the giveaway was small.

It had taken over one year to timestamp 500,000 blocks to the BAY Blockchain:

Block #500,000 (Reward 1.16867584 BAY) November 29th 2015 at 05:21:36 AM UTC

As 2015 drew to a close, Bjørn Alsos wanted to see a marked increase in activity on all BitBay related social media accounts. He admitted not enough people were working on the project, so it had suffered over the last year. He reminded the community that a major marketing campaign would not begin until most of the main features of the bespoke market client (out of beta) were ready. He said:

"No point introducing end users to an unfinished product!"

On New Years Day, there was renewed optimism within the community that 2016 would bring greater success. A major focus of attention was technical testing of the code. David Zimbeck was still the lead sole developer.

Throughout the entire year of 2015, the market capitalisation of BitBay never surpassed US$500,000. There were rumours that big initial investors of BAY had been selling frequently during the year, therefore keeping the price down. Whether this was the case or not, it could not last indefinitely. Two charts below show how the BAY market capitalisation fluctuated during 2015:

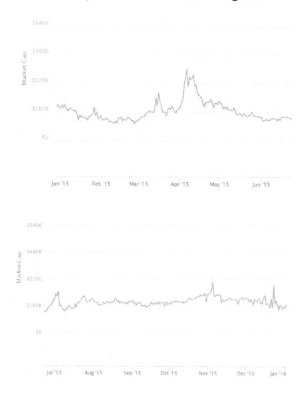

Towards the end of March 2016, work continued to develop the first official (not beta) market client before its release. Enhancements were being made to make it more secure and reliable. All issues reported by testers were in the process of being fixed, especially ones relating to the Windows compatible market client.

On the 3rd April, the BitBay market capitalisation, the value of all BAY units of account generated to date, surpassed US$500,000 for the first time since the 6th December 2014. As can be seen below, the Bitcoin Satoshi prices per BAY unit of account had roughly doubled on Bittrex over the last week:

	Bitcoin Satoshi price per 1 BAY (BAY/BTC)				
	Low	Open	Close	High	Volume (BAY)
28th March	78	88	92	92	4,542,846.41
29th March	85	92	87	92	3,336,177.80
30th March	87	87	100	110	10,710,651.22
31st March	88	100	92	101	3,393,436.23
1st April	88	92	103	130	6,959,646.85
2nd April	93	103	112	140	13,998,010.82
3rd April	112	112	162	150	11,802,999.96

SOURCE: www.cryptocompare.com

A major announcement was posted on the 5th May 2016. After much deliberation, the release of the next market client update (official public release) had been postponed indefinitely. They wanted to wait until the Windows, Mac OS X and Linux versions were all ready. They also wanted to wait until the "Buy/Sell Coins" template was complete. Help was requested from willing people to test the new beta versions. Bug bounties were offered and bug reports accepted as posts on either the official BAY Bitcointalk forum thread or the BAY Slack "client" channel.

David Zimbeck had been working tirelessly to develop Mac and Linux compatible market clients. Both had successfully passed testing phases. As regards the Windows version, only minor bugs were found and were then easy to fix.

Craig Claussen was instrumental during tests on the beta software. He gained a reputation for finding flaws in the code which others overlooked. He was described as finding approximately 75% of all code bugs so far.

On the 5th June, a video was uploaded to YouTube during which time Pirate Larry interviewed David Zimbeck. It lasted for nearly two hours.

I.   BITBAY MARKET CAPITALISATION SURPASSED US$1,000,000

II.   MARKET CLIENT VERSION 1.24 RELEASED ON 5TH DECEMBER 2016

III.   MARKET CLIENT VERSION 1.25 RELEASED ON 7TH JANUARY 2017

IV.   HARD FORK KICKED IN ON 21ST JANUARY 2017

V.   BITBAY PRESS RELEASE PUBLISHED ON BITCOINPRBUZZ.COM

5

BITBAY BLOCKCHAIN HARD FORKED TO PoS 3.0

"2017 is going to be the year worth watching BitBay very closely! After the next update, if we can get the price and volume to increase, everything will start falling in place and you will see one of the greatest 'underdog' comeback stories in the history of crypto!" - Craig Claussen

As part of a growing social media presence, the BitBay team created an official BitBay YouTube Channel on the 18th November 2016. A description of the project on that channel is as follows:

"Hundreds of features, Unbreakable Contracts, Decentralized Markets, Joint Accounts, Exotic Spending, IMAP and Decentralized Email, Multisignature with Steganography, Pay To Email, Voting, Locktimes, Barter, Employment, Cash For Coins, Python Contracts, Smart Contracts, Freezing and Unfreezing, it even translates to 92 languages...

and unlike other projects Bitbay has been market tested for 3 years. The software is robust and not vaporware, we deliver a real product. Welcome to the future of finance."

YouTube allows BitBay to upload content such as promotional videos, help tutorials and other relevant material. It is also another useful method by which to advertise the vision and scope of the project.

On the 24th November 2016, according to www.coinmarketcap.com, the market capitalisation of BAY surpassed US$1,000,000 for the first time since the 25th November 2014. It had remained below US$1,000,000 for almost two years!

Ten days later, the all time high 2016 BAY market capitalisation was reached at roughly US$1,298,664.

Both these milestones are represented in the following table:

	1 BAY BTC Sat	1 BAY US$	BAY Market Cap US$
24th November 2016	135	0.001000	1,000,000
4th December 2016	168	0.001290	1,298,664

SOURCE: www.coinmarketcap.com

On the 5th December, a transcript of an interview with David Zimbeck was published on Steemit.com and medium.com for anyone to read. David Zimbeck was asked about a dozen questions. One question and answer was:

QUESTION

Can you walk me through your vision for BitBay?

ANSWER

"I was on the team when BitBay still consisted mostly of undeveloped ideas. I was already working on decentralized markets with BitHalo, and the guys who brought me in just had a coin and a marketing plan. The original idea for BitBay was an international market, much like EBay. Unlike EBay though, BAY could be used to exchange anything, including the purchase of good and services, negotiating contracts, employment, and even in bartering. Also, unlike EBay, there are no fees. Perhaps most importantly, BitBay will be developed as a secure way for two entities to make any kind of unbreakable contract without the need for anyone else to be involved... no arbiters... no middle-man. This unbreakable contract technology was already a feature I built into BitHalo the year before. I was able to simply integrate it into BitBay."

Also on the 5th December, Bjørn Alsos announced that the new market client (version 1.24) was available for download. It included fixes to underlying network connectivity issues. Users who had not experienced any connectivity issues did not have to update. He went onto say:

> "For those of you that are new here: BitBay has two wallets, QT and client. Atm QT is the only one that can stake, and the client has all the cool stuff like smart contracts, market and pay to email. QT will be abandoned as soon as the client can stake, and is therefore not updated."

BitBay thought, with the increased attention lately, that it was important to release version 1.24 quickly so new users did not have trouble connecting.

It had taken 769 days to generate 1,000,000 BitBay Blockchain blocks:

Block #1,000,000 (Reward 30.0281656 BAY) December 18th 2016 at 09:16:16 PM UTC

On Christmas Day 2016, David Zimbeck was testing the code ready for the next market client release (version 1.25). It would be mandatory to install it.

Craig Claussen, BitBay Applications Manager from the USA, was enthusiastic for 2017. He was quoted as saying:

> "2017 is going to be the year worth watching BitBay very closely!
>
> After the next update, if we can get the price and volume to increase, everything will start falling in place and you will see one of the greatest 'underdog' comeback stories in the history of crypto!"

The last block timestamped to the BitBay Blockchain during 2016 was:

Block #1,017,024 (Reward 0.29583091 BAY) December 31st 2016 at 11:58:08 PM UTC

On the first day of 2017, the first recorded BAY market capitalisation was roughly US$928,207 according to www.coinmarketcap.com. Corresponding Bitcoin Satoshi and US Dollar prices per BAY unit of account were 96 and 0.000922 respectively.

On the 4th January, the all time low 2017 BAY/BTC price was recorded at 73 on Bittrex. What follows are the Bitcoin Satoshi prices per BAY unit of account on that exchange for the first four days of 2017:

	Low	Open	Close	High	Volume (BAY)
1st January	89	94	95	100	1,603,318.49
2nd January	94	95	98	108	2,008,679.48
3rd January	96	98	96	102	1,592,055.97
4th January	73	96	96	100	3,623,428.94

SOURCE: www.cryptocompare.com

During 2016, the BAY market capitalisation increased from approx. US$150,000 on the 1st January to approx. US$930,000 at the end of December. This was a percent increase of over 500%. Investors in the project were obviously euphoric.

Two charts below show how the BAY market capitalisation fluctuated during 2016:

On the 7th January, in preparation for the transition to proof of stake 3.0 (PoS 3.0), David Zimbeck posted an important update. Users were required to update to either version 1.2 of the core QT wallet client (Windows, Mac OS X or Linux) or to version 1.25 of the market client ready for the scheduled hard fork in two weeks time. A description of proof of stake 3.0 was also given:

> "1 billion plus 1% annual growth from soon to be POS3.0 stake reward. POS3.0 is much better than its predecessor. It enforces that no matter what 1% will be added to the coin supply - that's based on every coin staking. Since it's impossible for every coin to stake you earn more than 1% because you are reaping the reward that the current unstaked coins would be generating as well."

Once again, advice was given to only download software from official sources. All software would automatically handle the hard fork on the 21st January 2017 if and only if correctly installed.

Also on the 7th January, a planned press release on BitcoinPRBuzz.com was discussed. They politely requested 1.4 BTC to make this possible (0.6 BTC had already been raised). They appreciated help to achieve this target, however small.

On the 21st January at approximately 00:00 UTC, the network protocol seamlessly hard forked to the new parameters. Each and every block after block number 1,043,111 would generate a static 1.5 BAY reward (see below). Three other exclusive features included in the update were:

1. **Voting**—ability to use one's stake in BAY to vote on many issues.

2. **Cold Staking**—ability to put the highly secure wallet keys on two separate systems (not fully active in this update, but progress made towards it).

3. **checklocktimeverify**—allows one to automate what happens with one's BAY units of account at a future time (not fully active at this time).

Block #1,043,111 (Reward 13.54043142 BAY) January 21st 2017 at 12:01:36 AM UTC

Block #1,043,112 (Reward 1.5 BAY) January 21st 2017 at 12:01:52 AM UTC

During February, two press release articles relating to BitBay were published. They were welcomed by the core team and wider community as a way to promote the project to a larger audience.

Firstly, on the 1st February, an article titled "BitBay, from Violent Storms, to Safe Habor" was published on http://bluemagic.info/. It was described as covering the dramatic past, exciting present and enticing future plans. It can be read in the appendix of this book from pages 78 to 80.

Secondly, on the 13th February, an article titled "The World's Most Advanced Cryptocurrency Software, BitBay Makes Itself Visible" was published. It was the press release at http://bitcoinprbuzz.com/ promised after 1.4 BTC had been raised. It can also be read in the appendix from pages 81 to 83.

In reference to the second article, Bjørn Alsos said:

> "That is the press release. We also have an article that will be posted on 400+ sites and also translated to many languages
>
> A big thank you to all that contributed to this"

He was also happy to announce there was a greater focus on marketing. He notified the community that the BAY team had expanded to help with this endeavour. A highly professional video producer had been hired to create tutorial videos, which were nearly complete. Promotional videos were also in the works. Another individual referred to as gjsteele had also joined the team. He had proven himself to be a talented writer and marketeer. Bjørn Alsos wanted to add more members to the team, but only if they demonstrated the right credentials.

During March, insights into what will be included in the next market client (decentralised smart client version 1.26) were regularly posted. These updates included many features to make the market client more secure and user friendly. Five major features were discussed:

- **Cold Staking**: permits the user of the market client to store their keys on two separate systems. This is a security feature which makes it nearly impossible for people to compromise the user's wallet and manipulate their balance.

- **Client Staking**: renders the need to have both the core QT wallet and market clients running simultaneously obsolete. Users will have the choice to unlock the market client for staking BAY units of account.

- **Anti-Keylogger**: prevents anyone from recording the keystrokes used by a user when they enter their password.

- **Decentralised Voting**: ability to use one's stake in BAY to vote on many issues.

- **Tor Proxy**: masks the IP address for any market client related Internet requests. It was described as one more feature which places the user's privacy and peace of mind above the rest of the competition.

Version 1.26 of the market client was already available, but not yet public. Tests were being carried out to perfect the code.

On the 21st March, Bjørn Alsos praised David Zimbeck by saying:

> "I have talked a lot with David the last two years. The one thing he has said over and over, is that he will continue to develop to make sure the investors get what they paid for originally. And that's what he has been doing. And he has added a lot as well. Like anti-keylogger in this update.
>
> Thank you David for your persistence, your generous software, and most of all - your big heart. Bay is now finally rising like a Phoenix "

I.   MARKET CLIENT VERSION 1.26 RELEASED ON 22ND MARCH 2017

II.   FIRST BITBAY DECENTRALISED VOTING POLL OCCURRED

III.   BITBAY MARKET CAPITALISATION SURPASSED US$50,000,000

IV.   TRADING INITIATED ON CRYPTOPIA EXCHANGE

V.   OFFICIAL BAY TEAM GREW TO TWENTY FOUR PEOPLE

6

BITBAY TEAM FORMATION

"Recruitment for blockchain/crypto projects is a new and evolving process. Many organisations are still in their infancy in terms of being established and candidates can be naturally wary of providing long term commitment to a sector that government(s) and the media seem to have a love/hate relationship with." - Aletha Kellond

The second market client update of 2017 was released on the 22nd March. To be specific, it was version 1.26. It contained an assortment of features to make it more convenient, secure and private than ever before. Anyone who already had the previous client software installed were prompted to install the update as soon as they opened it. As highlighted over the past several weeks, the main features included in the second update were:

Client Staking – Moves PoS Staking to the Client, eliminating the need for the QT wallet
Cold Staking – Keep your two keys on separate systems safely securing your BAY
Anti-Keylogger – Enter password characters with your mouse instead of the keyboard
Decentralized Voting – Vote on anyone's proposal, or create your own
Added Tor Proxy – Utilize Tor for behind the scenes data retrieval

Other modifications were made cosmetically and in terms of ease of use.

During the previous week, the BAY market capitalisation had surged to new all time highs. BitBay entered the top fifty cryptocurrencies on the cryptocurrency ranking website at www.coinmarketcap.com as it surpassed US$7,000,000. What follows are historical figures from that website:

	Low US$	Open US$	Close US$	High US$	Volume US$	Market Cap US$
18th March	0.001832	0.002089	0.001882	0.002233	20,635	2,104,830
19th March	0.001838	0.001878	0.002136	0.002214	24,976	1,891,570
20th March	0.002106	0.002106	0.003608	0.004211	93,905	2,121,140
21st March	0.003663	0.003663	0.006724	0.007158	247,687	3,690,040
22nd March	0.004359	0.006911	0.005077	0.007524	193,050	6,962,150

On the 21st March, it was the first time that the overall daily 24h trading volume, over all recognised exchanges, had been recorded above US$100,000. This was further recognition that interest in BitBay had grown.

On the 30th March, the core BAY team announced the first official "BitBay Decentralised Voting Poll" to decide whether to fork to the correct BAY staking reward sooner rather than later. They admitted a mistake was made in the previous update from PoS 2.0 to PoS 3.0. Bjørn Alsos was quoted as saying:

> "When we forked to POS3 in January 2017, there was a glitch. The amount of coins was not adjusted, resulting in the stake being too low. It's now only 1.5 Bay for each block, but should have been 20.5 Bay. We used the built-in voting feature in our client to let the community decide if we should wait adjusting that until we fork for pegging, or if we should do it sooner."

Users had to install the market client to participate in the voting poll. They also needed BAY units of account to cast votes (0.000005554 BAY for each vote) either for or against an early hard fork. BitBay were proud to remain true to the decentralised protocol by hosting this voting poll. It would last for three days from the 1st April (07:00 UTC) to the 4th April (07:00 UTC). They were certain of further voting polls in the future.

On the 4th April, the first decentralised voting poll carried out on the BitBay Blockchain came to an end at 07:00 UTC. Craig Claussen announced the results:

"Voting results:
stakefork = 917 votes
nostakefork = 557 votes

Congrats! stakefork wins the vote!"

The organisers of the vote thanked everyone who had participated.

Investor interest in BitBay had continued to gain strength during April 2017. Its market capitalisation surpassed US$10,000,000 for the first time on the 22nd April. On that day at 09:20 UTC, it went on to reach a peak at roughly US$14,711,500.

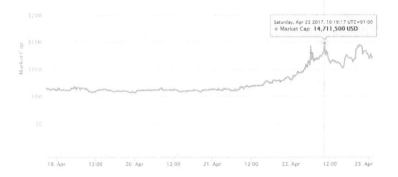

Historical data derived from www.coinmarketcap.com shows how quickly the US Dollar price per BAY unit of account increased, especially on the 22nd April. It was also the first time that both BAY/USD and BAY/BTC surpassed US$0.01 and 1,000 Bitcoin Satoshi respectively.

	Low US$	Open US$	Close US$	High US$	Volume US$
19th April	0.005447	0.006085	0.006016	0.006683	41,071
20th April	0.005716	0.006028	0.006192	0.006469	40,163
21st April	0.005893	0.006192	0.008479	0.008911	165,884
22nd April	0.008595	0.008691	0.012200	0.014676	514,100

On the 7th May 2017, about fifteen people were part of the overall BAY team. However, they thought the time was right to reorganise the structure of the team. A decision was made to announce vacant positions, except for Community Manager, for anyone to apply for. Some principal positions outlined were:

- **Head of Marketing**: to take BAY through the branding process and draw up a marketing plan. Experience with low marketing budgets required.

- **Marketing Assistant/s**: to assist the Head of Marketing.

- **Web Developer/s**: to possess in depth knowledge of Wordpress and SEO.

- **Event Manager**: to organise social media events, giveaways and competitions. Must have strong knowledge about the market client.

- **Support Manager**: to build up the support system to help users with the client software. S/he must have good all-round knowledge of the software and cryptocurrency.

- **Marketplace Salesman**: to make sure the marketplace on the market client is populated with contracts.

- **Social Media Manager/s**: to manage all (or part of) social media accounts.

Other roles required by the team included writers, graphic designers, video producers and so on. In particular, they wanted to attract professional developers to help with future tasks relating to mobile wallet applications, web interface creation etc. They also said the following:

> "ALSO We are looking for people that don't necessarily fit in one of the above descriptions, but who think they can make a contribution anyway -either because of skills not mentioned here, or because they are quick on their feet and can get things done when they are handed a task. CONTACT THEM on Slack (usual way!!!)"

Applications had to be sent to Bjørn Alsos, also known as Sirlosealot on BitBay Slack. He wanted applicants to describe their skill set as accurately as possible and give an estimation of how much time they would be able to devote to the position.

On the 25th May, the core BitBay team were happy to announce the release of market client version 1.27. Craig Claussen announced the following:

"We are happy to announce the release of the new version of the BitBay Halo Client. This release mainly focuses on performance upgrades and fine tuning the Client's many features. It will allow David the ability from here on out to focus solely on coding the final features of the core build."

In addition, a promise was made to include the patch for fixing the PoS 3.0 staking reward in a future release. A static 20.76 BAY block reward was required.

Throughout June 2017, the formation of the "BitBay Marketing & Management Team" was in progress. Not everyone who joined the team would end up contributing to the project and driving it towards its vision to become a truly decentralised marketplace. Many have contributed very little, and have since left.

There are currently five members of the core BitBay team:

- **David Zimbeck** —the Lead Developer of the project.

- **Craig Claussen** —the Application Manager of the project. He also helps test the client software.

- **Bjørn Alsos** —the Community Manager of the project. He also focuses on user experience and adoption.

- **Shorn** —the Project Manager who is responsible for planning and co-ordinating the whole team of 30+ people.

- **Aletha Kellond** —responsible for recruitment and global sourcing.

All other members of the wider BitBay team can be seen on pages 22 and 23 besides their corresponding positions.

Meet the Team

Throughout the first half of 2017, the BAY market capitalisation grew from strength to strength. In the space of six months, it had increased from just under US$1 million to over US$50 million. As can be seen below, the Bitcoin Satoshi price per BAY unit of account increased approximately twenty times.

	Market Cap US$	BAY BTC Satoshi	1 BAY US$	1 BTC US$	1 ETH US$
1st January 2017	928,207	96	0.000922	976.37	8.46
21st March 2017	5,022,672	458	0.004986	1,096.82	44.18
22nd April 2017	10,100,928	817	0.010026	1,218.02	48.44
20th May 2017	20,307,947	1,020	0.020157	1,999.99	131.55
6th June 2017	30,892,727	1,086	0.030662	2,738.91	256.08
7th June 2017	41,376,021	1,443	0.041067	2,815.30	263.97
24th June 2017	53,166,016	1,949	0.052767	2,682.65	342.68

A market capitalisation peak was reached at roughly US$53,166,016 on the 24th June 2017. This would not be surpassed until the 16th November 2017. A chart derived from www.coinmarketcap.com below shows how the market capitalisation ascended to the peak:

On the 17th July, the BAY team were excited to announce the latest market client release. Version 1.28 was another performance update which made it possible for the development team to focus solely on coding new features to the market client. They were also improving the user interface (UI) templates.

After conversations on BitBay Slack, a decision was made to get BAY live trading initiated on another cryptocurrency exchange. Cryptopia was chosen as the "best bet", but 1.3 BTC was required to get added sooner rather than later.

One week later on the 21st July, the full 1.3 BTC had been raised. David Zimbeck promised to contact Cryptopia as soon as conveniently possible. Those who donated were highly praised:

> "Again, thanks everyone, we take pride in having a community that wants to see this project succeed. After all, none of this means anything without the community's enthusiasm and continued interest in bringing BitBay to life."

On the 28th July, Cryptopia initiated the BAY/BTC trading pair on their exchange platform. It's an exchange (as well as a marketplace and forum) based in New Zealand which offers deposits, trades, and withdraws of Bitcoin, Litecoin, and over 400 other cryptocurrencies. It went live on the 6th December 2014.

During Summer 2017, David Zimbeck was still working diligently to finalise the code ready for the future hard fork. It would increase the staking rate from 1.5 BAY to 20.0 BAY per block. Other objectives focused on the ability to freeze and burn BAY units of account.

Also, people were encouraged to fill in a recently created marketing survey. A 2,000 BAY prize was available for the person who could provide the best suggestion regarding BitBay's future marketing and development. It was accessible via the link https://bitbay.typeform.com/to/RHhm6b. The team had already analysed the data collected so far.

Silvervox325, and his team, were congratulated for moving BitBay up the SEO (Search Engine Optimisation) rankings.

On the 1st October 2017, a long awaited official BitBay Block Explorer went live at http://explorer.bitbay.markets thanks to the hard work done by two developers called Anoxy and GiorgosK. Unlike the explorer at https://chainz.cryptoid.info/bay, which went live on the 15th November 2014, it can be programmed to the requests of the community to show bespoke features. This event was described as the first step of the *"BitBay|Easy"* development line before the creation of the upcoming BitBay Web-based Wallet Application.

Also, we would like to thank you for reading this far and welcome you to become involved in our fast-growing community.

WWW.BITBAY.MARKET

BitBay had grown substantially in terms of value, the size of its official team, the number of supporters and its outreach. Twenty four people were now part of the recognised "BitBay Marketing & Management Team". As always, people were encouraged to join the conservation on social media platforms, notably Slack and Telegram. Updates and announcements on Reddit and Twitter were becoming more frequent week by week. A new roadmap detailing future scheduled plans was being devised.

On the 7th October, Craig Claussen was quoted as saying:

> "The marketing team is growing stronger day by day. We are completing
> a lot of tasks that don't always get noticed. It will continue to grow. Over time
> we will include frequent press releases, and continue the task of making this
> user friendly to the 'normies' so that we can go full force marketing mode
> to the world rather than just the crypto speculators."

Other events which occurred during this period included:

- On the 26th June, the all time 2017 Bitcoin Satoshi high was reached at 1,995 on Bittrex.

- On the 28th June, an official Discord Channel was created for BitBay. The community were notified that Slack will still be the best source for support and breaking news.

- The total number of registered members on the BitBay Slack Channel had grown to over 1,000 on the 30th June.

- On the 7th July, Blocknet successfully tested an atomic trade transaction between BitBay and DigiByte.

- The BitBay Telegram Group went live on the 13th July.

- On the 16th September, David Zimbeck successfully tested the first BAY checklocktimeverify (CLTV) transaction.

- On the 3rd October, an AMA (Ask Me Anything) discussion happened on the official Ark Slack Channel at 10:00 PST. It gave supporters the opportunity to ask David Zimbeck and Bjørn Alsos intriguing questions.

I. NEW BITBAY ROADMAP UNVEILED ON 8TH OCTOBER 2017

II. MARKET CLIENT VERSION 1.29 RELEASED ON 1ST NOVEMBER

III. BITBAY WEB WALLET RELEASED ON 27TH NOVEMBER

IV. HARD FORK KICKED IN ON 30TH NOVEMBER

V. MARKET CAP SURPASSED US$100,000,000 FOR THE FIRST TIME

7

MARKET CAPITALSATION AND MARKETING SURGE

"We are sincerely grateful to everyone who has been a part of BitBay in the past year. From users, to investors, to team members both past and present—thank you!" - BitBay Team

Marketing and promotion were growing day by day. As part of the vision going forward, the "BitBay Marketing & Management Team" were proud to unveil a revamped roadmap on the 8th October 2017. It was described as invaluable after the recent growth of the project. It outlined key objectives to look forward to.

Team members had been coding and rebranding BitBay. These included:

- Bruno Guimarães (BitBay Art Director) was working to design the upcoming revamp of the official BitBay website.

- GiorgiosK had assisted in styling the recently created BitBay Block Explorer.

- Shorn had worked hard to make the official BitBay website suitably match new fonts, graphics and other branding styles.

- Anoxy had worked to develop the upcoming BitBay Web Wallet.

Just before the roadmap announcement, the official BitBay website experienced some sort of attack. Preventative measures were thereafter put in place. What follows is the roadmap infographic:

Other key events which occurred during October 2017 were:

- It was reported that someone had successfully sold five acres of land situated in Southern California to a buyer in Norway using the market client. The seller later joined the BitBay team.

- On the 24th October, a South Korean exchange called UPbit added BAY to their platform besides 114 other cryptocurrencies. This was also the day on which they launched in open beta testing mode.

- The number of people visiting the official BitBay website and downloading the wallet client software had grown considerably over the last few weeks.

On the 1st November, the "Exotic UI Spend" update was released. To be more specific, version 1.29 of the market client and version 2.0 of the core QT wallet client were ready for download. It was a mandatory requirement for users to update immediately so that they would not miss the upcoming hard fork at approximately 00:00 UTC on the 30th November 2017.

This update included "Exotic Spending" features. In simple terms, it allows the user to create time based contracts by using checklocktimeverify (CTLV). Some examples of how it can be useful are:

- **Dead Man's Switch**: ability to return BAY units of account to their rightful owner after a predetermined time locked period.

- **Notary and Burn**: ability to verify the ownership of documentation.

- **Freezing Coins**: ability to create savings accounts and futures markets.

On the 20th November, the community were notified that the official BitBay website at https://bitbay.market/ had been relaunched after a successful revamp. User "BitBaydev" was quoted as saying:

> "A big thank you to everyone who has helped make this happen and we've really appreciated all your feedback and suggestions over the last few months. Community is what we're all about at BitBay and the new website is a perfect example of ours working together."

On the 27th November at 19:00 UTC, the BitBay Web Wallet was released. It marked step two out of seven of the *"BitBay|Easy"* development line that kicked off with the launch of http://explorer.bitbay.markets.

It allows users to send, receive and store BAY units of account without the need to synchronise (download the full blockchain onto one's computer). It is a standalone application and can be easily integrated into websites for payment services. It was designed for speed, simplicity and security.

On the 30th November 2017, the scheduled hard fork occurred at block number 1,448,465 without any problems. It was the second hard fork of 2017. The BitBay Blockchain transitioned to new parameters and fixed the staking rate. From now on, each and every block would generate 20 BAY units of account.

Block #1,448,464 (Reward 1.5 BAY) November 30th 2017 at 12:00:32 AM UTC

Block #1,448,465 (Reward 20.0 BAY) November 30th 2017 at 12:00:48 AM UTC

Work continued to market BitBay to a larger audience. People were encouraged, with the availability of BAY bounties, to translate official material into other languages. Constructive talks were also being made with public relation firms to promote the project in the mainstream commercial sphere. The number of people following the official BitBay Twitter account (@BitBayofficial) had grown from 8,000 to 9,000 in the last week alone.

On the 4th December, the new BitBay Community Support Portal went live at https://forum.bitbay.market/ where all support documents, user guides and video tutorials can be found. There is also a FAQ section there.

Investors and supporters were ecstatic after witnessing how quickly the BAY market capitalisation had ascended. It had increased to an all time 2017 high of ~US$340,912,738 on the 19th December 2017. At this high, the corresponding US Dollar and Bitcoin Satoshi prices per BAY unit account were 0.338085 and 1,772 respectively. Historical figures derived from www.coinmarketcap.com were:

	Low US$	Open US$	Close US$	High US$	Volume US$	Market Cap US$
16th Dec	0.088150	0.088240	0.116278	0.132003	20,677,900	88,971,000
17th Dec	0.111385	0.113377	0.128398	0.141556	11,903,000	114,320,000
18th Dec	0.124115	0.129740	0.246230	0.263578	34,713,700	130,821,000
19th Dec	0.223786	0.276697	0.264587	0.338085	50,906,500	279,011,000
20th Dec	0.212705	0.259951	0.272943	0.280766	20,646,200	262,132,000

BitBay surpassed Syscoin in terms of market capitalisation on the 19th December:

63	BitBay	$340,912,738	$0.338085	$42,780,300	1,008,363,986 BAY *	163.99%	
64	Syscoin	$328,059,061	$0.619403	$15,861,500	529,637,508 SYS	22.82%	

Also on the 19th December, the number of people following the official BitBay Twitter account surpassed 10,000 (now over 17,000 followers).

Two days later, the number of subscribers to www.reddit.com/r/BitBay hit 1,000.

On the last day of the year, Bjørn Alsos wished everyone a Happy New Year. He highlighted the astronomical BAY market capitalisation surge. It had increased from approximately US$1,000,000 at the beginning of the year to approximately US$178,000,000 on the 31st December 2017. It was a great indicator that the project was attracting a larger pool of people.

BitBay had come a long way during 2017. The overall BAY team had grown from three very active members (David Zimbeck, Craig Claussen and Bjørn Alsos) to over thirty part/full-time members. Two successful automated hard forks took place, the BitBay rebranding process was highly praised, many innovative "crypto-first" features were implemented and the future looked more promising than ever.

> "The BitBay team wishes you a happy new year, wherever you are in the world. #2017 has been an interesting journey and we're sure #2018 will be even more exciting!"

APPENDIX

BITBAY, FROM VIOLENT STORMS TO SAFE HABOR

1st February 2017

In the cryptocurrency universe where people often make significant investments into ideas before the first line of code is ever written, one of the world's most secure currency projects has already released a major product.

You can't tell the story of BitBay without providing a brief bio about the developer David Zimbeck. When David started working on BitBay, he had already developed one of the first successful bitcoin based cryptocurrency projects called BitHalo. It provided a solution to remove the middleman from transactions. For the first time in history, Halo tech allowed for counterparties to transact in a truly trustless, peer-to-peer environment, without the need for a 3rd party arbitrator dictating who's at fault when a transaction goes sour. David's concept was the final piece to the puzzle of Satoshi Nakamoto's fundamentals of creating a peer-to-peer currency, removing the demand for intermediaries to keep people honest. Bitcoin posed a limitation on the BitHalo Client, which BitBay is able to overcome. The BitBay Halo Client's key difference will be to include a revolutionary price stability protocol to remove price volatility – yet still allow fluctuations – through a Client that holds both cold wallet security with hot wallet functionality.

The project is years ahead of any other decentralized smart contract system all in a 100% trustless environment. BitBay has a fully functioning client with so many capabilities it's best to provide a link to review them: https://bitcointalk.org/index.php?topic=1744745.0

Any arrangement you can come up with can be customized within BitBay's existing client. Do you want to exchange XMR for ETH without first having to convert to BTC? Are you interested in trading your silver dollars in exchange for gold krugerrands? Want to create a binary option with a trade buddy because you think the price of gold will increase to the US Dollar at a specific time? Want to buy BAY cryptocurrency with EURO? How is this possible? The solution is called Double Deposit Escrow, or Trustless Escrow. Simply explained, each party in the agreement puts up a deposit as collateral to assure the transaction is completed successfully. After all parties are happy, the deposits are returned.

This encourages each party to work out any issues and discourages scammers because they have no way to profit. There are no middlemen and no corporate fees... as a matter of fact there are no fees of any kind. It is completely FREE to use.

While there are many enhancements planned for the BitBay client to increase security even more and make it "mom-friendly," the contract creation system is live and stable. Cold staking, price pegging, and keylogger defense are important and ambitious additions planned for 2017. BitBay's cold staking feature allows users to create an account by installing two private keys on two separate computers. To break in and gain access to a user's account, a thief would need access to both systems, then to find the keys hidden in pictures (steganography encryption), and to unlock both keys. The upcoming release of price pegging will create the stability needed to utilize the powerful combo of blockchain and smart contracts in the real world.

There is arguably only one proven method of price-pegging, and it involves the freezing/unfreezing of a currency to control the inflation/deflation of the value. User accounts will consist of both frozen and liquid BitBay coins controlled by a decentralized algorithm along with the built-in voting system. The liquid coins can be used as an asset within the client to purchase, or as collateral for contracts. If the user value protection algorithm calculates the need for the total supply of the coins to deflate, then a portion of a coins in a user's account will freeze to weaken sell pressure on the exchanges. Even though small portions of your account could be frozen, these coins will still be able to be sold through a time-lock-verify futures market, and therefore can be exchanged for other assets in the market price.

Price-pegging is necessary for BAY within the BitBay client because people need a reliable store of value which will have the same or greater value in the future. On auction sites today, such as EBay, people sell in exchange for dollars or other national currencies, which will likely retain a similar value next week. For a crypto currency to be used in exchange for goods/services and as collateral for contracts, it needs to do the same.

The pegged value of BAY will be decided by voting using the Proof of Stake system already available, so the people with the most at stake will decide the price, which will also result in their personal BAY being frozen or unfrozen. This "rolling peg" will still allow the price to fluctuate somewhat but the extreme volatility we have become familiar with in crypto will not be possible. The price will roll gently like the gentle swells in a safe harbor, instead of being subject to the violent waves common to the vast ocean of cryptocurrency pump and dumps.

David has been working relentlessly for years and all the hard work should soon begin to finally pay off. He has overcome all of the early adversity and delivered everything he promised to the community in the tumultuous early days of BitBay. Rather than struggling to recover the stolen coins taken by the ICO exchange host, the community decided it would be best to keep the decentralization of BitBay intact to maintain the principle of cryptocurrency. For over the last 2 years, Lin Han of Bter, has been dumping his coins to deter investors' confidence and dishearten David's ambitions for the project. Without the proper funding due to the ICO thievery, marketing BitBay to the world has been extremely challenging. The good news is that we've been tracking Lin's accounts since the beginning and as our price charts are starting to show, he has run out of his supply, finally allowing for the market to correct to a fair price. At this point the "million dollar question" is the discovery of what the true fair market price really should be!

The Worlds Most Advanced Cryptocurrency Software, BitBay Makes Itself Visible

13th February 2017

Bitcoin Press Release: *BitBay cryptocurrency software suite offers state-of-the-art contracts and marketplace solutions.*

February 13, 2017, Baja California, Mexico – BitBay, the cryptocurrency software suite offering unbreakable smart contracts was keeping a low profile for some time but has now resurfaced; stronger than ever. The creator and soul developer of BitHalo/BlackHalo David Zimbeck has worked effortlessly the past two years to create the most advanced and secure wallet in cryptocurrency space. The software suite is capable of supporting an entire smart contracting interface with decentralized markets and other features.

A BitBay community member comments,

"How is it that a single developer can deliver such an incredible suite when entire teams of coders have a hard time even delivering a functional wallet? How on earth has this project gone unnoticed, and why is it not in the top 10 coins in the world?"

Unbreakable Smart Contracts

Unlike many other platforms, BitBay is not vaporware. It is a feature rich platform that offers unbreakable smart contracts for important real world applications. The BitBay contracts are far superior to other smart contracts as they are secured by collateral deposits from both parties, which makes it unbreakable. In the event of a default by one of the parties, their collateral funds will be burnt, making it illogical for them to cheat or exit the contract with the intention of defrauding the other.

The smart contracts system on BitBay eliminates arbitrators, biased third parties, escrow and even fees. Without any middlemen, it can create coins for cash contracts like a decentralized "LocalBitcoins", where cash payments are completely trustless. It can also be used to create "employment contracts", "decentralized eBay-like delivery contracts" (to ensure prompt delivery of working products), and even "barter contracts" that allows people to create a "wish list" and trade any item off that list.

The user-friendly templates on BitBay enable users to create smart contracts by just entering few details. The platform currently has a handful of templates in place, with more to be added shortly. In David Zimbeck's words, all one has to do is use their imagination to create a custom template for any deal they want. The platform's "Cash for Coins" template has already been successfully used by many to automate buying process and complete cash deals without needing escrow or middlemen. The platform will soon release a "buy/sell anything" contract template with reverse and regular auctions support. It will also include a variety of shipping choices.

Decentralized Marketplace

BitBay had a decentralized marketplace almost a year before "Open Bazaar". BitBay's completely anonymous market is built right into the client, and it allows users to create their own public and private markets. Or they can just check different contracts already available in the main market. The BitBay software allows communication between users by supporting email with end to end encryption like Thunderbird and it also supports Bitmessage for a more decentralized option.

Other features on BitBay include "Pay to Email" which uses steganography to hide payments within photos sent to recipient's email. The feature, originally created for tipping purposes has various other applications as well.

Even the wallets' two encrypted keys can be hidden within images using David's steganography based feature. These keys can then be used on two different computers to sign transactions – a feature that lays the foundation for "Cold Staking", which will be utilized in both BitBay and BlackHalo. The Cold Staking feature will be almost impossible to crack because the computers used to sign your transactions can be in completely separate locations. BitBay will also make allowance for "exotic spending" such as "locktimes". In addition to the "dead man's switch", "parking of coins", "burn" and other spending types, it also supports automated joint accounts for business partners and spouses. The BitBay platform can also translate to 92 different languages.

About BitBay

BitBay has so far created a whole cryptocurrency ecosystem with its own functional market economy. All these things have turned BitBay into a powerful cryptocurrency software suite that can take on other cryptocurrencies. The platform enjoys a vibrant community that is regularly attracting and training new users. The "contract faucet" created by one of the team members is currently giving away coins using a unilateral "Guarantor" contract to whoever accepts it.

BitBay will soon release their secret star feature that will eliminate the cryptocurrency's volatility.

Learn more about BitBay at – http://bitbay.market/

Media Contact

Contact Name: David Zimbeck
Contact Email: dzimbeck@gmail.com
Location: Baja California, Mexico

BitBay is the source of this content. Virtual currency is not legal tender, is not backed by the government, and accounts and value balances are not subject to consumer protections. This press release is for informational purposes only. The information does not constitute investment advice or an offer to invest.

www.ingramcontent.com/pod-product-compliance
Lightning Source LLC
Chambersburg PA
CBHW071305050326
40690CB00011B/2535